Peg Digs a Dam

By Debbie Croft

Peg met Bec at the dam.

The rams can not
get in the dam!

Peg gets in the cab.

She digs up the mud.

Peg digs and digs
at the dam.

It is a big job.

She gets hot!

Bec can see Peg is hot.

Bec digs a big dam
for the rams.

It is a big job!

The rams get hot.

The rams get in the dam!

The dam is big.

Peg and Bec get in the dam!

CHECKING FOR MEANING

1. Why did Peg have to dig a dam? *(Literal)*

2. What did Bec do when Peg was hot? *(Literal)*

3. Why did Peg and Bec get in the dam with the rams? *(Inferential)*

EXTENDING VOCABULARY

dam	Look at the pictures in the text and explain what a *dam* is. What other words do you know for places that hold water? E.g. pool, river, ocean, sea, pond, creek.
big	Which word in the text rhymes with *big*? If you change the *i* to an *e* in *big*, what word do you make?
job	What is a *job*? If you put the letter *s* at the end of the word, how would its meaning change? Can you use this word in a sentence?

MOVING BEYOND THE TEXT

1. What other big machines are used on farms or at pits?

2. What are dams used for? What smaller animals live in dams?

3. Why is it important to drink water on a hot day?

4. Why is Peg wearing a hard hat when she is digging?

SPEED SOUNDS

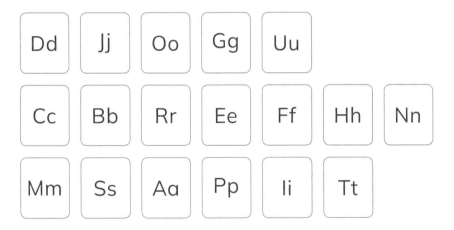

Dd	Jj	Oo	Gg	Uu

Cc	Bb	Rr	Ee	Ff	Hh	Nn

Mm	Ss	Aa	Pp	Ii	Tt

PRACTICE WORDS

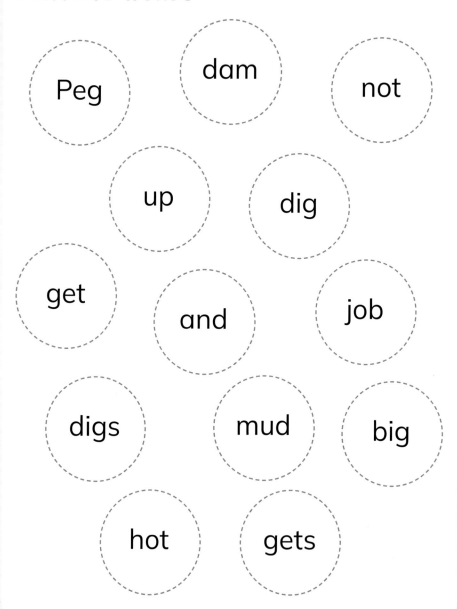

Peg

dam

not

up

dig

get

and

job

digs

mud

big

hot

gets